CB

6/15

D1501949

MONSTROUS MYTHS

Terrible Tales of the
MIDDLE AGES

Clare Hibbert

Gareth Stevens
Publishing

Please visit our website, www.garethstevens.com. For a free color catalog of all our high-quality books, call toll free 1-800-542-2595 or fax 1-877-542-2596.

Library of Congress Cataloging-in-Publication Data

Hibbert, Clare.
Terrible tales of the Middle Ages / by Clare Hibbert.
   p. cm. — (Monstrous myth)
Includes index.
ISBN 978-1-4824-3299-2 (pbk.)
ISBN 978-1-4824-0193-6 (6-pack)
ISBN 978-1-4824-0191-2 (library binding)
1. Tales, Medieval — Juvenile literature. 2. Civilization, Medieval — Juvenile literature. 3. Folklore — Europe — Juvenile literature. I. Hibbert, Clare, 1970- II. Title.
GR78.H53 2014
940.1—dc23

First Edition

Published in 2014 by
Gareth Stevens Publishing
111 East 14th Street, Suite 349
New York, NY 10003

Copyright © 2014 Arcturus Publishing

Illustrations: Janos Jantner (Beehive Illustration)
Editor: Joe Harris
Designer: Emma Randall
Cover designer: Emma Randall

Printed in the United States of America

CPSIA compliance information: Batch #CW14GS: For further information contact Gareth Stevens, New York, New York at 1-800-542-2595.

CONTENTS

MEDIEVAL STORIES

During the Middle Ages, people looked at the world in a way that would seem pretty strange to us today. Many ideas that we see as fantastical, they took very seriously. For them, witches, giants, curses, and talismans were all very real!

In books about animals, creatures such as elephants and lions were listed alongside dragons and unicorns. Travellers' guides described foreign lands populated by dog-headed people and headless people with faces in their chests.

Medieval stories often featured menacing monsters—such as the Laidly Worm.

The Church was very powerful, but Christian beliefs were mixed with ideas that we would now call superstition. There were very few books, as they were all hand-copied manuscripts. But hardly any people could read anyway! They learned Bible stories by listening to sermons.

Storytelling was a popular pastime. Everyone would gather to hear tales of mermaids, goblins, bloodthirsty wolves, and man-eating giants. In these stories, things were not always as they seemed. For example, the famous Laidly Worm was really a princess under a spell.

Other legends tried to make sense of recent history. Across Europe, nobles were capturing land and creating new kingdoms. Real battles and power struggles were turned into exciting stories where knights were honorable heroes bound by the rules of chivalry, fighting wicked villains.

Believe it or not!

Medieval doctors weren't like today's. Top treatments included bleeding patients or making them throw up. No wonder people preferred to rely on spells to cure their illnesses!

GEORGE AND THE DRAGON

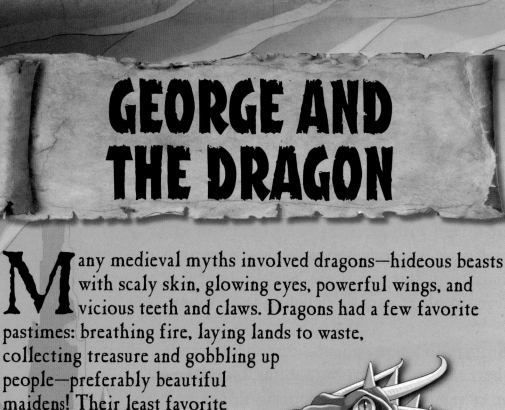

Many medieval myths involved dragons—hideous beasts with scaly skin, glowing eyes, powerful wings, and vicious teeth and claws. Dragons had a few favorite pastimes: breathing fire, laying lands to waste, collecting treasure and gobbling up people—preferably beautiful maidens! Their least favorite pastime was being slain by gallant knights.

The dragon was an evil, bloodthirsty monster that could breathe fire.

George was a gallant knight travelling through the Middle East. When he reached the land that is now Libya, he met an old hermit. The hermit told him that a wicked dragon was ravaging the land surrounding the town of Silene and stopping the townspeople from collecting water from the nearby spring. Not only that, but the dastardly dragon demanded a human sacrifice every day. Only girls would satisfy his horrible appetite, and now the town was down to its last one!

Typical dragon behavior – they're such fussy eaters.

The last remaining girl in Silene was the king's daughter, Sabra. She was due to be handed over to the dragon the next day. Of course, when fearless George heard this, he was determined to save the princess.

George sought out Sabra in the dusty valley near the dragon's cave. At the sound of horse's hooves, the dragon flew out. When it saw George blocking the route to its princess picnic, the dragon roared a deafening roar and flapped its scaly wings threateningly.

Undaunted, George galloped at the dragon with his lance in one hand and his shield in the other. He lunged at the beast's scaly skin, but it was too tough.

Again George tried to attack the dragon, but this time it spat poison that burned right through his armor. On his next attempt, George aimed his weapon at a weak spot in the creature's hide, where there were no scales. He penetrated the beast's flesh easily.

George relied on his religious faith...and his trusty lance!

Quick as a flash, George called to the princess to throw him her girdle (a kind of belt). He slipped it around the dragon's neck to make a collar and lead. Then George and Sabra led the wounded beast back to Silene like a giant-sized, fire-breathing Labrador! The king was overjoyed to see his daughter still alive. It must have made for a quite an entry in Sabra's diary...

Dear Diary,

What a day! Instead of being digested by a dragon, I've been given another chance at life. And it's all thanks to gorgeous George!

There's just one problem: when my dad offered George a reward (such as my hand in marriage, hint hint), he started talking about a foreign religion instead! He says he'll kill the dragon if everyone converts to something called 'Christianity'. Dad seems keen on the idea – he's promised to build a church once the dragon is done for.

Believe it or not!

George really did exist. He was a Roman soldier and a Christian. Unluckily for him, he served during the reign of Diocletian (284–305 CE), an emperor who hated Christians, and he died a martyr.

THE LEGENDARY KING

Arthur must be one of the most famous English kings, though it's not certain he ever really existed! But whether or not he was a real king, his life story has become the stuff of legends.

Arthur's father was bold Uther Pendragon, king of Britain. He brought the standing stones to Stonehenge from Ireland, with help from the wizard Merlin. But not even Merlin's magic could save Uther from being poisoned.

Uther's death was followed by dark times for the Britons. However, at least baby Arthur was safe. Merlin had taken him far away, to be brought up in secret.

Only the rightful king, Arthur, could break the enchantment that held the sword in the stone.

Arthur grew up without having any idea that he was a prince. He was serving as a page for a knight called Sir Ector when Merlin came to find him. The wizard took him to a churchyard where there was a sword set in a stone. The sword was inscribed: "Whoever pulls this sword from this stone is the rightful king of all England." Many had tried but there was no budging the sword—not until Arthur came along, that is!

To Arthur's astonishment, the sword simply slipped out! Merlin promised to serve Arthur just as he'd served his father before him. On hearing of Arthur's feat, the most powerful nobles in the kingdom swore to follow him.

King Arthur quickly became famous for his bravery and his awesome skills as a warrior. He couldn't perform magic like Merlin, but some of his deeds seemed just as superhuman!

Not everything was rosy, though! Plenty of people wanted to seize the throne from Arthur.

One day, Arthur and Merlin were riding past a lake on the island of Avalon. A hand rose from the water, holding a sword in a scabbard! Merlin encouraged Arthur to row out to the sword and grab it. The trusty sword, known as Excalibur, made Arthur an even more powerful fighter.

Merlin guided Arthur towards the magical sword, Excalibur.

Every king needs a queen, of course, and Arthur chose the lovely Guinevere. As a wedding gift, Guinevere's delighted dad sent Arthur a circular table. Arthur loved it! He gave it a place of pride at Camelot, his castle, and chose his best warriors to sit around it. The Knights of the Round Table swore to be true to Arthur.

Arthur's reign didn't please everyone. He had some relatives who didn't believe in family loyalty. Morgan le Fay, Arthur's half-sister, was a sinister sorceress. She was always plotting against Arthur, his knights, and his queen.

Arthur's nasty nephew, Mordred, turned out to be even more of a problem. When Arthur had to go abroad to fight, he left Mordred in charge—but in Arthur's absence, treacherous Mordred made himself king. When Arthur returned, there was a battle. Arthur killed Mordred, but was himself mortally wounded. He asked one of his knights, Sir Bedivere, to come with him to return Excalibur to the lake where he'd found it. As Arthur died, a mysterious barge appeared and whisked his body away.

Believe it or not!

The Great Hall is all that remains of the medieval castle in Winchester, England. It is home to a painted tabletop that is said to be the Round Table. However, it dates only to the 13th century, not the sixth, when Arthur was said to be king.

THE GREEN KNIGHT

One New Year's Day, an unwanted visitor appeared at Camelot—the Green Knight. He didn't just have a strange name. He was actually lizard-green all over! Clutching a festive sprig of holly in one hand and a lethal battle-axe in the other, the knight issued a challenge. Someone could behead him with an axe—but he would return the "favor" a year later.

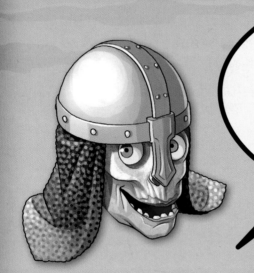

I don't think much of the Green Knight's festive spirit. New Year parties don't usually include a beheading contest!

Young Sir Gawain took on the dare. With a confident swing of the axe, he lopped off the Green Knight's head. End of story! Well, not quite... Astonishingly, the knight picked up his severed head from the floor and strode out of the hall. At the doorway, he cheerily reminded Gawain: "See you this time next year! I'll meet you in the Green Chapel."

The next November, Gawain mournfully set off to find the chapel. Along the way, he encountered wolves, dragons, and giants. He slept in his armor, so that he was ready to face any danger.

Just after Christmas, Gawain reached a castle and was welcomed in by its lord, Bertilak. Gawain discovered that he was close to the Green Chapel now. He could rest and prepare for his encounter with the Green Knight. To pass the time, Bertilak suggested a game—he and Gawain would swap whatever they were given each day.

On the first day, Bertilak went hunting deer. Back at the castle, Gawain was teased and flattered by the lord's pretty wife. Being a knight, he couldn't be rude to a lady or disloyal to a host. Eventually he let her give him a peck on the cheek.

To everyone's surprise, the beheading didn't kill the Green Knight!

That night the lord gave Gawain venison from the hunt. In return, Gawain passed on what he had received that day: a peck on the cheek! It was a similar story the next evening. Bertilak presented Gawain with a wild boar, and Gawain gave him two kisses.

On the third day, the lady went to Gawain just as he woke, terrified, from a nightmare about the Green Knight. As well as three kisses, she gave him her magic green girdle, which she said protected the wearer from death. That night, Bertilak handed over a fox he'd killed, but Gawain returned only the three kisses and not the girdle. Oops. Cheating was a big no-no in the age of chivalry!

How could Gawain hope to survive when he had promised to let the Green Knight strike him?

16

The next day Gawain set out for the Green Chapel. He was too honorable to run away—even when he heard the dreadful sound of the Green Knight sharpening his axe! Amazingly, the knight missed with his first and second blows, and only nicked Gawain's neck with the third.

Gawain couldn't believe his luck—until the knight revealed that he was really Bertilak. The mastermind behind the beheading contest was King Arthur's witchy half-sister Morgan le Fay, out to cause trouble as usual. The two misses were for the first two days of the swapping game, Bertilak explained, when Gawain had honestly handed over the kisses. The tiny cut was his punishment for keeping the girdle.

Although he'd shown himself to be brave, Gawain returned to Camelot as red-faced as the knight was green-skinned. From then on, he wore a green sash as a reminder of his weakness.

Believe it or not!
The famous Irish hero Cuchulain was also tested by a "beheading contest." His opponent was a giant disguised as an old man.

QUEST FOR THE GRAIL

Many legends grew about the court of King Arthur and his Knights of the Round Table. The most extraordinary of all was the quest for the Holy Grail.

It all began when Sir Gawain arrived at the court with a message from Merlin. The poor old wizard had been trapped inside an oak tree by the Lady of the Lake. This powerful sorceress had once been Merlin's student, but she was hardly a teacher's pet! After Merlin had taught her all his magic, she used it against him.

Merlin knew that no one could save him. However, he could offer Arthur one last piece of advice. He told him to send his knights to find the long-lost Holy Grail. This was the cup that, according to Christian tradition, Jesus drank from at the Last Supper.

Arthur hosted a jousting tournament and feast to celebrate having all his knights together before they scattered to find the Grail. During the feast, there was a dramatic peal of thunder, and then light poured through the castle windows.

Many sporting contests have cups as prizes. The Grail was the greatest prize of all!

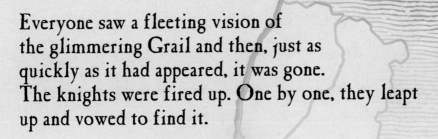

Everyone saw a fleeting vision of
the glimmering Grail and then, just as
quickly as it had appeared, it was gone.
The knights were fired up. One by one, they leapt
up and vowed to find it.

Sir Perceval was the first to encounter the Grail. On his quest
he met an old fisherman who offered him a bed for the night. The
fisherman turned out to be a king! His kingdom had been under a
terrible curse ever since a knight called Sir Balin wounded him,
and it wouldn't recover until someone healed those wounds.

*The Fisher King had been
wounded in combat. All
that he could do was fish!*

The Fisher King invited Perceval to dine at his palace. As servants paraded past with dazzling dishes, Perceval spotted the Grail among them. But poor Perceval, distracted by the food, missed his big moment. Instead of having his eyes on the prize, he had his eyes on the pies!

The Grail's powers would have healed the Fisher King's legs and brought prosperity back to the kingdom. But the moment passed, the Fisher King remained lame, and the next morning, the palace vanished into thin air.

How did Arthur's other knights fare on their quest? Let's imagine their letters home...

Arthur, my king,

I tracked down the Grail! But then I fell into a daze and it vanished. How weird! I think it was because my heart's not pure. I'm really not sure why...

Dutifully yours,

Lancelot

P.S. Might it be because I am in love with your wife?

Would any of Arthur's knights prove themselves worthy of the Grail?

Your majesty,

Great news! Galahad and I have found the Grail. Goody-two-shoes Galahad is obviously pure of heart, so that probably helped. But I also proved myself in a test along the way. I had to choose whether to save my brother or a damsel in distress, and I went for the maiden. It was a no-brainer, really, though family Christmases might be a bit sticky from now on!

Yours, Bors the Younger

The knights never managed to take the Grail back to Arthur. In a vision, Galahad was instructed to transport the cup to the island of Sarras. He was made king there—but now that he'd seen the Grail, he didn't want to stay in the world any longer. Angels carried him up into the clouds, along with the Grail, never to be seen again.

Believe it or not!

Just as Arthur's knights hunted for the Grail, heroes in Celtic folklore quested for a magic cauldron.

BEOWULF

Beowulf was a square-jawed hero with an appetite for adventure. His father was the king of the Geats, a people who lived in what is now Götaland, southern Sweden. One day, Beowulf heard news of a terrible monster that was terrorizing the king of Denmark. Here was Beowulf's chance to make his name as a monster-slayer! He rounded up a group of warriors and set off.

The monstrous Grendel had brought terror to the people of Denmark.

In Viking society, kings and lords built great halls where their warriors could feast, drink mead, and listen to stories. Hrothgar, the Danish king, had built his men a hall, but the sounds of their merriment had upset a demonic swamp creature. Grendel was a terrifying sight—less-than-human, misshapen, and savage. For 12 years, Grendel had treated Hrothgar's hall like a self-service cafeteria. Each night, he turned up and devoured another couple of Danes.

When Beowulf arrived and offered to rid Hrothgar of the evil beast, the king was delighted. That evening, the warrior entertained the Danes with tales of his brave deeds...but could he live up to his boasts?

When the men were all sleeping, Grendel appeared and wrenched open the door. More fearsome than Beowulf had imagined, he killed one of the Geats before Beowulf could stop him. But then Beowulf began to fight—without any weapons—and he proved stronger than the monster. As Grendel struggled to escape, Beowulf ripped his arm from its socket. The demon limped away to die, while Beowulf hung up the blood-soaked arm as a trophy.

You could say that Grendel was now mostly 'armless!

Grateful King Hrothgar showered Beowulf with treasure, weapons, armor, and horses. The celebrations continued long into the next night. But while the men partied, Grendel's grief-stricken mother was closing in. That night, as the men slept, a creepy creature slithered into the hall and snatched Aeschere, the king's right-hand man.

Grendel's mother was a kind of wicked water creature. She had made her lair at the bottom of a deep, dark lake.

Beowulf vowed to destroy Grendel's monstrous mom, and he and his men followed her trail across the fens. On a clifftop, they reached the sorrowful sight of Aeschere's severed head. Below them, in the murky waters of a huge lake, they saw sea dragons and serpents. But that didn't scare Beowulf, who dove in—armor and all.

At the surface, Beowulf's followers waited and waited. Eventually, they spotted blood bubbling up from the depths. Some of them left then, sure that Beowulf was dead. But a few stayed on and soon saw a very welcome sight—their master surfacing, victorious! He'd cut off the monster's head with a giant-sized sword he'd found in her lair!

Beowulf returned home a hero. He became king of the Geats and ruled for 50 years. He did have one last monstrous adventure. When he was an old man, an angry dragon began to terrorize his kingdom, scorching the earth with its fiery breath. Beowulf fought and killed the dragon, but suffered a fatal wound. Death by dragon bite was the perfect end for a larger-than-life hero!

Believe it or not!

There's no evidence that Beowulf himself existed, but there is evidence that Hygelac, named in the story as Beowulf's uncle, was a real Geatish king.

OUTSIDE THE LAW

The legendary hero Robin Hood first appeared in stories toward the end of the Middle Ages. It was a time when people were facing real-life baddies instead of dragons and mythical beasts.

Medieval life was tough if you were at the bottom of the heap, especially if people higher up the food chain were corrupt. In Robin Hood's day, the Sheriff of Nottingham was one such villain.

The sheriff worked for the king—but which one? England had two, sort of. The real king was Richard I, a warrior so courageous that he was nicknamed "the Lionheart." While he busied himself with battles abroad, he left his brother John in charge.

That John was a nasty piece of work. He wanted the throne for himself.

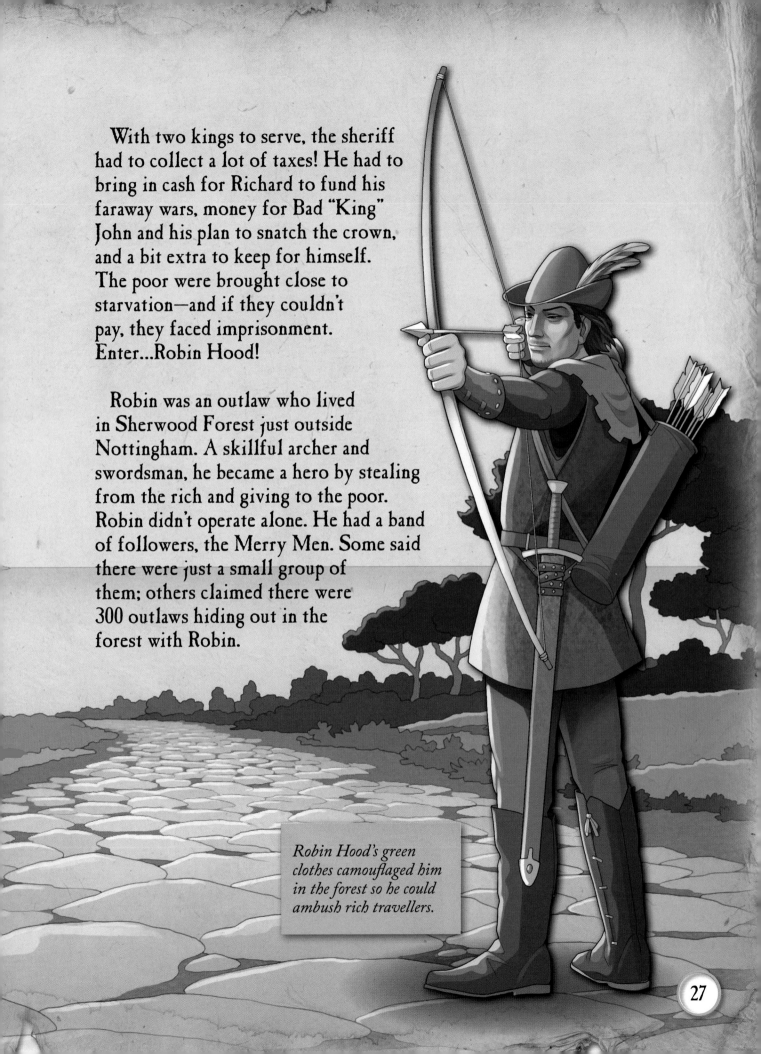

With two kings to serve, the sheriff had to collect a lot of taxes! He had to bring in cash for Richard to fund his faraway wars, money for Bad "King" John and his plan to snatch the crown, and a bit extra to keep for himself. The poor were brought close to starvation—and if they couldn't pay, they faced imprisonment. Enter...Robin Hood!

Robin was an outlaw who lived in Sherwood Forest just outside Nottingham. A skillful archer and swordsman, he became a hero by stealing from the rich and giving to the poor. Robin didn't operate alone. He had a band of followers, the Merry Men. Some said there were just a small group of them; others claimed there were 300 outlaws hiding out in the forest with Robin.

Robin Hood's green clothes camouflaged him in the forest so he could ambush rich travellers.

Robin's second-in-command was loyal Little John, whose name was a joke—this beanpole towered over seven feet (two meters) tall! Another member of Robin's band was Much the Miller's Son. Much was a big, beefy fighting machine, who had been given a death sentence for deer poaching, The best swordsman was Will Scarlet, a noble on the run after killing his dad's wicked estate manager. Friar Tuck was the chubbiest but, despite his size, he was a formidable opponent.

Robin experienced Friar Tuck's sword-fighting skills. The two got into a fight when they first met!

Whenever Robin got into trouble, he blew three times on his hunting horn and his men rushed to his rescue. Headstrong Robin often ventured into Nottingham and put himself in danger. Sometimes the wicked sheriff captured Robin, and the men had to stage a jailbreak. Cunning Little John was the brains behind these missions.

Robin and his men were constantly outwitting the scheming sheriff, who spent much of his time thinking up ways to take his revenge and have Robin hanged. Those plans, and his plans for raking in money, took up most of his time, but not all. He had room for one more obsession: beautiful Maid Marian. The sheriff was determined to marry her, even if it meant doing so against her will.

Robin had other ideas. Braving the sheriff's guards and then the sheriff himself, he broke in, rescued Marian, and carried her to safety. Marian married Robin, joined the Merry Men, and turned out to be almost as good an archer as Robin was!

Believe it or not!

According to researchers, the real Robin Hood may have been Robert fitz Ooth, the 12th-century Earl of Huntingdon, or a 14th-century Yorkshireman called Robert Hood.

GLOSSARY

archer Someone who shoots arrows from a bow.

Camelot The name of King Arthur's castle and court.

chivalry The moral code that medieval knights were meant to follow. It involved being brave and courteous.

fen Low-lying, marshy land.

girdle A belt worn around the waist.

hermit Someone who has decided to live alone, away from society, usually for religious reasons.

Holy Grail According to Christians, the cup that Jesus drank from at the Last Supper (his last meal with his followers or disciples before he was put to death).

hunting horn A musical horn used to give a signal to others when hunting.

jousting A medieval combat sport for knights on horseback.

lance A very long weapon with a sharp head, used when charging on horseback.

manuscript A handwritten piece of text. In the Middle Ages, books were hand-copied and often decorated with beautiful pictures or patterns called illuminations.

martyr Someone who dies or is put to death for their religious beliefs.

mead An alcoholic drink made from fermented honey.

outlaw Someone who is living outside the law.

page A boy in training to become a knight, who learned what he needed to know by being the knight's servant.

poaching Stealing game animals, such as rabbits, pheasants, or deer, from someone else's land.

prosperity Success and good fortune.

quest An adventurous journey in pursuit of a particular object or goal.

scabbard A sheath for a sword.

standing stones Large stones, positioned in prehistoric times, that had religious importance. The ring of stones at Stonehenge were arranged there around 5,000 years ago.

superstition A belief based on the idea of supernatural forces bringing good or bad luck.

talisman An object like a charm, believed to have magical properties, stop evil, and bring good fortune.

FURTHER INFORMATION

Further Reading

The Adventures of Robin Hood by Marcia Williams (Walker, 2007)

The Adventures of Sir Gawain the True by Gerald Morris (Houghton Mifflin Harcourt, 2013)

Arthur, High King of Britain by Michael Morpurgo (Egmont, 2008)

Beowulf by Kevin Crossley-Holland (Oxford University Press, 2013)

Dragonslayers from Beowulf to St George by Joseph McCullough (Osprey, 2013)

Medieval Myths, Legends, and Songs by Donna Trembinski (Crabtree, 2006)

Websites

www.bbc.co.uk/programmes/b00p1msk
The BBC's online guide to its popular program set in Arthurian times, *Merlin*.

www.bl.uk/onlinegallery/onlineex/englit/beowulf
The British Library's online exhibit of the Beowulf manuscript, including an audio clip of the poem being spoken in the original Old English.

www.boldoutlaw.com
A website devoted to all things Robin Hood.

www.historyforkids.org/learn/medieval/literature/beowulf.htm
A guide to Beowulf with some useful recommendations for further reading.

www.storynory.com/2009/12/14/sir-gawain-and-the-green-knight-part-one/
An audio version of the first half of the Gawain story; visit the Storynory homepage to find part two.

INDEX